The Way I See the World

By Yasmin Latif

Age 12

Copyright © Yasmin Latif 2015

All rights reserved. No part of this publication may be reproduced, stored in a retrieval system, or transmitted in any form or by any means, electronic, mechanical, photocopy, recording or otherwise, without prior written permission of the copyright owner. Nor can it be circulated in any form of binding or cover other than that in which it is published and without similar condition including this condition being imposed on a subsequent purchaser.

ISBN 978-0-7552-8000-1

Book produced and published by
Bookcreateservice Ltd
www.bookceateservice.com

Contents:

Introduction: 5

Is Aspergers A problem? 9

What is the Meaning of 'people?' 11

Believe in Yourself 13

Who We Are? 14

Is There Such a Thing as a Best Mum? 16

The Sparkling Wind Chimes 18

The Shining Red Beach 20

Happy Days Montessori Poem 22

The Magical Tree 24

The Boy in the Garden 26

Google Chrome 27

Respect 28

Satisfaction: 29

Negativity 30

The Mind 31

Roots 32

Love 33

Doveland 34

Love 36

The Joy of Peace... 37

Fear 38

The Peaceful Garden 39

Introduction:

Hi my name is Yasmin Latif and I'm 12 years old. I was diagnosed with High functioning Aspergers syndrome when I was 7 years old. At first Aspergers affected my life very strongly and I feel that the environment I was in didn't help. Up until I was 8 I grew up in a very negative environment where my mum and dad weren't happy together and of course that affected me even more. Seeing my parents unhappy caused me to feel very unsafe in my environment, which made me lock myself away from everything 24/7. I didn't know how to express myself in an appropriate way so decided to scream, kick and shout whenever I felt like it. This caused a lot of stress to form between me, my mum and my dad which made it even harder for me socialise in an appropriate way. We were all stuck inside our own comfort zone not knowing what to say, think, or do at what moment.

In the middle of all this I was homeschooled at my mum's Montessori nursery in Wembley from the moment I was born. When I was 5 or 6 my mum made a Montessori primary class for me and 6 other children where we all learned the Montessori materials. When I was 7 I decided I wanted to go to primary school and so my mum sent me to a private primary school round the corner from her nursery. It ended up that I didn't fit into that environment either because I was too different from the other children and shook a piece of paper which I call a string, so it ended up being that they didn't understand me either, so my mum decided to home school me again. My mum brought in a fully qualified teacher for me to work with which continued until I was nearly 10.

Between all of this my mum and dad decided to separate and for me and my mum to move out. My mum had a flat that she had rented out since I was 2. When I was 8 I decided I wanted to go to school again so my mum sent me to a state primary school where I had an LSA. They understood me a lot better than the private school but when I was 9 I decided I wanted to be homeschooled again, so my mum brought me back to her nursery again. Then when I was 11 I decided I wanted to go to secondary school. For the first 2 weeks I loved it but then I began to dislike it and so changed back to being homeschooled again. I have been homeschooled ever since and probably will be up until college please God.

Now I have a tutor who comes to my mum's nursery on Monday, Tuesday and Wednesday to teach me geography and science. Geography is my favourite subject. If you gave me a sheet of flags I would tell you the names of all of them. When I was 9 I decided to see how I was at writing poetry. I wrote 5 or 6 poems when I was 9 and continued writing poetry when I was 11. One day when I was studying English with my mum, one of the activities was to do a poetry project and stick it up in your school hall. So my mum and I decided that I should make a poetry project and stick it up in the Brent civic centre. So we went and asked them If I could stick it up in the children's library and they said "no" because it didn't have the Brent logo already printed on it. So we contacted the Ealing road library and they stuck it on a poster at the entrance to the library. I left it there for 3 weeks to show how children with Aspergers can do anything they want just like everybody else.

Then my aunty Ellen and her colleagues at her work Tait studio organised a fundraising event for children with Aspergers called "how am I wired" to prove that all people are wired differently. In the middle of all this I thought that I should make my very own poetry book. So we contacted my uncle and he got a publisher for me. Then it was a matter of doing this Introduction, sorting out the contents page and organising all the poems in order. So as I said, I have a big interest in poetry and that's how this fabulous book came about.

In this book I've used a mixture of acrostic, cinquain and sensory poems for you to enjoy. All these types of poems have touched and formed an interest in me, so I thought I could put them in this book for you to explore. Poetry has become a wonderful part of my life. Every time I read a piece of poetry that I'm interested in, I dive into the personification of the poem. I feel like I'm a person walking through this wonderful land full of wonderful things to explore.

I really hope my book brings awareness to you, that children with Aspergers can do anything and that all people are wired differently. I also hope you will enjoy a fabulous journey through this book please God. "Enjoy".

Yasmin

June 2015

Is Aspergers A problem?

What do you think Aspergers is?
Something silly, weird and hard to deal with?

What about you?
Have you got anything that's different to the few?
It might be something that's
Never been diagnosed.
Not liking maths or even prose
Or wanting to lie in bed all day
And blow your nose.
Those things have certainly not been diagnosed.
But it might be something that you are.

If you've got something like that or something similar to it
It only means its part of you.
Something that is unique to you and not bad in any way,
It's basically you and that's what Aspergers is it's a way of life; well that's what I say.
And not something bad and hard to deal with.

Today people think it's a condition to get flustered and frustrated about.
But it's not it's a way of life not something to make you shout

Aspergers is actually so easy to deal with.
But you won't get through to the child with anger and frustration.

You will only dump that precious moment in the building of your relation.
However once your soul is connected to the child through love.
Then all the good things will happen and you'll fit like a glove.

So whoever says that a child with Aspergers can't socialise or do anything that other people can do are wrong.
Because Aspergers is a way of life that's affected by bad energy and not by a song.
The outer energy affects the inner energy of the child with Aspergers and that's what causes all the chaos inside the child to come out.

Adults and children with Aspergers are very clever you know
They might even be cleverer than you something they would never show
You may be the one that's locked up in your head
Not the child with Aspergers who you think is stuck like lead.

What is the Meaning of 'people?'

What do you think people are?

Do you think they're things that always have a scar?

Well I think people are things that have a bright soul

Full of universal power that it's so easy to create a goal.

But most people cover that soul with hard balls of clay that are so hard to break through.

Most people make up any old excuse

To say that life is so hard to live.

But it's not once you start to give.

Give to yourself and others all that love inside of you and all that kindness and happiness with not a slight bit of pretence.

So that you're not pretending to give out that love so that people will think.

"Wow that person is really caring."

No that's not what you do because you're only pretending to yourself not to anyone else.

So now give that a go

And I promise you you'll see a difference and certainly a bit of cleverness.

But in order for it to make you feel great you have to do it with a positive thought.

I know I've got so much love inside of me and I am going to show it

To people in a good positive way for their sake and my sake.

Believe in Yourself

Don't let things hurt your feelings

It's no use when you're not believing

When people hurt you let them try but don't cry

When you're stuck with something hard don't let it feel like lard

So always believe in yourself

And always think I am myself.

Who We Are?

If somebody asks you what's your name what do you think

Do you think of it really quick?

Or do you go all shy and don't explain why.

Well when somebody asks me I think of it straight away

Not let it stuck in my head like a ball of clay

I undo the ball of clay really quick

And throw it into the other person's head

Now I don't want to talk anymore just not interested I suppose

Maybe it's because I'm different with a different soul

So bright that it's very easy for me to score a goal

You see everybody's different even your own relatives

But there's one thing you can never change about people

And that is everybody's got a heart of gold that is always shining

But people cover it with anger and fear and the sad thing is that you can never help them if they don't try because they hold the key to it themselves.

So always remember you can't help someone if they don't unlock the door to it,

And you hold the key to yourself so if you want to change then change.

Is There Such a Thing as a Best Mum?

If you're asking me if there's a such thing as a best mum

My answer would be 'definitely' because I have one myself

And the one I have is amazing with such a lovely body which has

A lovely face that's never sad because it's always laughing and smiling

And she has a lovely heart and soul which is always shining brightly

With an amazing golden light that you can feel all the happiness that's inside

And I love that body heart and soul because it's never empty of piercing bright gold.

And that body does everything with love; never with anything else.

Her love is so strong that I cry inside when I do anything wrong.

It's such a spiritual heart that it shines directly into mine.

I think that's why I want to be an archaeologist when I'm older so that I can pick out sparkling stones that give out that spiritual feeling.

So I love her very much for all those things and even more reason's that I can't explain.

And again that's why when I do anything not very nice to her I cry inside. So why do you think your mum is a special mum to you?

The Sparkling Wind Chimes

I peeped out the window and saw the wind chimes sparkling on the tree

I knew they were calling me.

I stepped outside and said take me to Neverland

At that moment a magic swirl took me into fairyland [Neverland]

The ground was covered in deep snows.

And people were shooting their frosted bows

Just then I saw an Artic fox with a white fur body

So unique he didn't look like anybody

I hugged him with the best of love and it reminded me of a Dove

I walked away slowly and he sounded growly

I threw him a piece of fish from my pocket and put it in a bucket

I stood there looking at the sea

And knew that this moment was meant for me

I began to feel the love and security of God

And suddenly a butterfly came out of the air and I put it in a pod

The magic swirl took me back to my house

And I was carrying a Mouse.

The Shining Red Beach

One morning I woke up with a start to see my granddad holding a picture bursting with art.

I looked up at him to see his gleaming red outfit

And on it a picture of the London Designer outlet

Where have you been granddad I asked?

Oh somewhere very special that even has a magic kettle

And where is that I asked

Oh its planet Mars darling and I met this guy called Willy Wonka

Are you sure you didn't dream this I asked

100% sure and come on so I can prove it

So I went outside and looked around and there

Was a shining red beach with a complete red sea

Oh I surely wish mum was here I said, she would honestly be shocked

And at that moment mum appeared

I really thought I was dreaming I stretched my arms out as

Wide as they would go and dropped myself in the freezing cold sea

It felt like ice everywhere I touched

Well said grandpa what do you think

It's all planet mars, it's all the powdery stuff that's on it with craters all around

And I made it happen with the help of Willy Wonka

Wow I gasped its good enough to sleep on and that's what we're doing with your mum tonight.

Then I stepped on to the sand with delight

Where an Ice cream was waiting for me

I ate it feeling so thrilled of what I had discovered.

It was a wish I always wanted to come true and so it has and it proves to me there's a God everywhere you look

Who's always happy and full of loving energy.

Happy Days Montessori Poem

Come and visit happy Days Montessori

They're always reading a story.

The principal loves to look at Wayne Dwyer

But she hates a busted tyre.

Come and visit Usma she's very caring

But sometimes she can be very daring.

Come and visit Shayma and

What about Anula.

Come and visit Shital she's very healthy

And also very jolly.

What about Abrine she dresses very nicely

And speaks very kindly.

Oh and katey as well she buys things too much

But brings back a very nice lunch.

And what about Humaira she drinks tea to much

And also Renew she wears jeans a lot and is very cute.

What about Yasmin she loves going on the tube

But she's not very artful and last of all

The children they are all so very peaceful.

The Magical Tree

I was in a forest park and all around me was very dark

I peeped behind a tree and suddenly it began to sparkle

I looked into my pocket and found a piece of mackerel

Then I hugged the tree

And it started to talk to me

I jumped back with fright and it began to shine so bright

Then I ate my mackerel and just then it began to sparkle

I said I better go to sleep and it began to feel like sleet

The next morning I woke up to find a breakfast on the table

And just then I saw a cable

I touched it carefully and then I stepped back nervously

I said I better go now tree; will you miss me?

Oh very much Indeed so here's a gift would you like a lift?

Oh it's ok tree once you love me

Yes I surely do and there's the gift for you

I began to walk home and on the way I saw a gnome

When I arrived home I sat in the lounge on the sparkling couch.

The Boy in the Garden

The garden was as cold as ice
So there was no sign of any mice
The ground was as white as snow
That I thought it was about to glow
I shivered with the cold
And for a moment thought that I was bold
I dreamed of hot chocolate and drinking it under the stars
While looking up at planet mars
I was almost sure I was late for school but I decided to play a game of pool
So I went inside to start the game
When suddenly I heard my name
I took a deep breath and looked up to see uncle Aiden
He stared down at me with such a lovely smile
That I just stood there for quite a while,
He stood there and said I'm a bit cross with you for
Being late for school but I also would love to play a game of pool,
Then he said I have something to say
And that is I love you either way.

Google Chrome

Google chrome is a very fast server but as with

Every server you might get some murder

You can go on YouTube and look up things to do with a cube

And what about looking up about facts, you might

Find things about different acts

Why not go on Amazon

You might buy a lot, but always carry on

So Google chrome

Isn't bad and it certainly won't make you sad.

Respect

When I walk into someone's house or even my house
We shouldn't act like a mouse.

We should show respect to the people and their house
Even if we don't like them [or it]

Because they like it [for themselves]
And they would feel sad and it would make me [or us] feel bad
Even if we're bad ourselves

Because they are themselves

And if they change they would look [act or feel] strange

Satisfaction:

The trees are bare.
While the birds are singing

Have satisfaction in your heart
And you will see a better start

We are always doing
We do not give ourselves a chance
To sing out that beautiful flower of light

Just look out your window and see what's around you
Just stop doing all the time.

Negativity

Your negative is the plant that's dying

Your soil is the candle that's flickering

The trees are dying while the snow is flickering

The Mind

Your mind will let you feed
But always remember to happy breath.

Let it out with light
And find a better sight.

Roots

Your roots are in the mud
And your soil is above
The water is splashing while your soil is shining.

Love

Love is bright
Love is light
Love is the way we begin our life

Love is the way we end of life
Love is in the sky

Love comes from very very high in the sky
Birds and animals always have love
And they show it when they sing

Love is like bright gold
From a brand new ring

Doveland

One day I saw a dove and as always it was full of love.

It just stood there peacefully in the tree reaching its soul out to me.

Suddenly I saw a fairy; I thought it must be the fairy of love.

Just looking at her fitted for me like a glove.

As I looked at the dove the fairy lifted me off the floor and through a magic door.

As my body sparkled I transformed into a fairy dressed with stunning clothes

Just fit for me; now I knew this moment was meant for me.

Suddenly I was led to this amazing land and presented with a sparkling wrist band.

The message just came into my head that I had been inside my very own soul

Looking at each and every goal

I flapped my wings and flew past a waterfall

With splashes falling beneath it that were so powerful

A magical candle appeared in front of me

The candlelight was glowing with love and that made the journey fit for me just like a glove.

I thanked the universe for this wonderful gift that made my heart lift.

I thanked the universe for this wonderful gift

That made my heart lift.

Love

Love is red

It sounds like golden light

It tastes like sweet cakes

And smells like blossoms

It looks like a red pond

It makes me feel like a soft white dove

The Joy of Peace

Peace

Nature's friend

Mankind's special key

A sign of candlelight

Stillness

Fear

Fear is black

It sounds like solid block

It tastes like rotten insects

And smells like sewer

It looks like a black desert

It makes me feel like a black solid stone

The Peaceful Garden

Gardens so full of nature

Animals running from a stranger

Rakes digging in to the ground

Dogs running all around

Echoes singing in the wind

Nature is our greatest friend

www.ingramcontent.com/pod-product-compliance
Lightning Source LLC
LaVergne TN
LVHW021743060526
838200LV00052B/3444